Ross Leckie

The Authority of Roses

For Fred, (Wah)

The words are

a hollow body.

Ross Leckie

Brick Books

CANADIAN CATALOGUING IN PUBLICATION DATA

Leckie, Ross, 1953-
The authority of roses

Poems.
ISBN 0-919626-90-4

I. Title.

PS8573.E3377A88 1997   C811'.54   C97-930327-3
PR9199.3.L42A88 1997

We acknowledge the support of the Canada Council for the
Arts for our publishing programme. The support of the
Ontario Arts Council is also gratefully acknowledged.

The cover is courtesy of Sue Schenk.

Occasional engravings are courtesy of Albert F. Moritz
from his book *America the Picturesque
in Nineteenth Century Engraving.*

Typeset in Trump Mediaeval.
Printed and bound by The Porcupine's Quill Inc.
The stock is acid-free Zephyr Antique laid.

Brick Books
431 Boler Road, Box 20081
London, Ontario, N6K 4G6

I 2 3 4 • 99 98 97

For my father,
Robert G. Leckie 1913-1995

and for my mother,
Doris J. Leckie

Contents

I.

Water Finding Its Own Level

During the Fall

For John Reibetanz

Rain: imagine the word standing
in this ethereal glade, and listen
to the hours patter on networks
of spiring overgrowth, as if each leaf
holds the limit of water's solidification.
When an icy juice discovers its
capillary surge through the fibers
of your shirt, it clamps to your chest,
to the small of your back. It curls
along an eyelash and splatters
when you blink. Focus the droplets
that string themselves on webs,
gather in blossom gullets, or
distend along a single razor
of grass. Soft beings bend gently
to the weight. No keen thing
remains so in this thick air.

Breakwaters

The stick sluices through the breach of matted leaves,
a tumbling buoyancy, a quickening. I put it there.
I couldn't bear the rain's mindless superfluity,
the way it runnels in seeming perpetuity,
next to the curb. Shaping the turgid mass
of mud and mulch into long spindly spits
that reach across the street, or dredging dams
that hug the waters as if they were industry
on the verge of economic collapse and decline
toward unemployment. Will I be an engineer
when I grow up? The currents now race
and there eddy, then sidle left or right,
looking for passage where they might condense
and collect with other water, seeking its level,
the placid espoir of the planet's mythology,
final quietude in ocean and thickening seas.
I place another twig into the snatch and thrust,
watch it chute through the roil, then slow,
follow it through a system of locks and canals,
thinking the grandeur of liquid conduit,
Amazonian dugout, primitive canoe, a Volga
boat song, steamer churning up the Congo,
St. Lawrence laker freighted with leftover ore.
It wanders into the sewer. I glance into that simple hole
which gurgles like the phantom of the opera.
Currents change and breakwaters erode, slide, suspend,
submerge – the street returns to its routine. It's time
to turn from this river, this local run-off
and its parish curriculum. I'm late for school.

The Runner

Where the distance between two points
is a circle, the runner reacquaints
himself with diversion. This curricular
antinomy he allows himself. You are
meandering somewhere when he slaps
by, heading around the block, counting laps.
If you consider it, he isn't in the least
surprising to you yet you are released
from your own footfall, left to
count the steps of the runner who
has disappeared around a corner.
He vanishes around the corner
as an act of self-effacement
and what remains is the placement
of figurines in a shop window.
The figurines suggest everything we know
about permanence and you suppose
it is the same runner as he slows
for a streetlight who has returned again,
focusing your attention upon the way some men
are embarrassed by their bodies. They glance,
as they tug at their shorts in a bewildering dance,
at the traffic that noses on its way
toward its employment. It is always today
for the runner whose force exerts
itself to little purpose. Still, the runner flirts
with tomorrow's contingency. If you know
the runner personally, you do not wave hello,
for his grim face is absorbed by what he isn't
doing. Though you are engaged in the pleasant
contemplation of a walk, the moment
he breezes by you your thoughts are rent.
You recognize that your strolling ends in death,
so it is you, not he, who stops to catch your breath.

The Watermelon

The brain is mottled green with dark green veins.
This once I wish to progress from this smallest infinity
to an infinitely smaller one. Let it have
the shape and gravity of a watermelon.
It must bear the gravid weight of an embrace.
The embrace must carry the weight of fear.
'It is only the wind,' I say.
The short man with the tooth-brush mustache
declares his anger. 'I am angry,' he declares.
Anger itself is red and slightly sweet.
To propose that one loves this person or that woman
is to create dusky categories; this flesh, this pulp.
Perspiration occurs in the operations of pumps,
clanging in the Jenkins Tap and Valve Company.
On this field behind the town in which we live
bodies bump like the awkward thump of the dropped watermelon.
A common insect life scrambles in the tepid air.
It is toxic where the sad creatures lie stunned.
These images of ridicule, slippery pips spit on the grass.
Meaninglessness contains such equality, dark
voracious space for every pipsqueak thought.

The River

I speak of the grace of the superfluous
not constituted in the arc of the rainbow.
A dandelion seed plopped out of the sun

and circled in the circling air into the circling
water of the stream. Surprise was
captured by the penitence of that gesture.

Flowering forward in the water's whorls,
it was carried away. It was a large cloud
or a tiny snowflake. It vanished.

The seed in the stream did not discover
the sheltering home of a fecund harbor.
Ice crystals proliferated their spores in a sheet

across the now-calm. Winter air expanded
water into the bubble of a contact lens, the weeds
imprinting their limp carcasses into the glass.

The sun was a pink eye. Constricted
twigs of the rose bush would not exhale,
but we spent our keening breaths.

Turning Once to Look Back

Last night I asked the stars to stop making that cricket noise.
Was it like the leaves shivering between moments of stillness?
Love prompted me to answer the ringing phone booth.
I think the wires rubbed themselves together
to make a strange sound, what she said
was only a scratch in my ear,
as if it were long distance.
I would like to say that I was weary, or world-weary,
but I felt fine, my loafers shone like new pennies.
It made me think of gases in the wheat fields,
of that other time,
the thankless thanatos in the wheat berries.

Onions

For A. F. Moritz

Its black core surprised you when you sliced
the onion. If you had peeled it layer by layer,
you would have uncovered each rind and its
milk, until there was no turning back. Is this
a parable of desire, our turning the pages
inked with an imprimatur of the book
we both read and write? Philomela,
lover of melody, creates balconies of the night
with the sound she makes. It was a lapse
of memory, an echo of another time.
If I were to visit the city whose map
I keep on my night-table, I would be lost
amongst a people whose language I do
not speak. Better to finger the lavish
boulevards and pursue them into traffic
roundabouts, skim past the magisterial gaze
of an unknown hero, arm extended, and
pointing toward the far-off edges of the city.
And let's remember these are false tears,
or induced by the pungency of the vapors
of an onion. I, you, what's the difference?
Neither is capable of slipping past the curvature
of the self, and I and you are fables of a talk
of endless mistaken identity. And the real you
doesn't know what to make of this invitation,
to enter by way of the you or the I or the we.
This is what you see when you rub the tear
from your eye, from the onion I've just sliced.
It is twilight and winter in the map of the city,
and people are bustling past the shops with the
expensive cheeses and breads, the sweets, the tortes;
others are huddled in the space between buildings.
The ominous sizzle is domestic, pleasurable,
and I, you, we, are thinking about dinner.

Aurora Before the Dawn

Let us say that God is unimaginable,
or figured only in a passion play of light
that criss-crosses through the upper air.
Ariel's song is bent by waves of gravity,
pulled earthward in the flare of sinking beauty.

At magnetic north, the needle spins
its breathless sweep across the rim.
It turns like an old song on the phonograph,
and in this undirected voice we know
exactly where we are in this polar cold.

Here the boreal aurora is a tent we stand inside,
its orangy nylon flapping slowly
in the solar breeze. The sky seems closer,
larger, as if the stars themselves were
tumbling in a shower of brilliance.

We do not live at the pole. We live off-stage
in lives whose rise and fall we try to plot
by actuaries, until, reminded of loneliness,
our heart's compass thrills to the earth's
flicker of attraction in deepest night.

At the Funeral
In memory of Harold Oldham

For an afternoon,
he pushed the canoe
upstream, the paddle
forcing its complex
of whorls into the water.

His muscles tightened
to the gunnel's thrust,
the canvas stretched
to a sprung rhythm
of tensile cedar

that slapped
across the waves
the way the flat of the hand
pats at the kneaded
bread. At a bend

in the river
he caught sight
of the expected thrush,
solitary on the
branch of a pine.

It offered no song,
and in the moment
that relaxation rippled
through, he let the canoe
come round to the

ebb's sinewed grip.
Whether it was
a giving up or a
giving over, he
couldn't quite decide.

Twilight in the Park

It is the definitude of the last thin shadows
of the man-child as he sings himself asleep
that separates the lost realm of noon sapphire
from the tightening glove of deeper shadow.

'Don't ask questions,' the wind says and it
hums and whines like a child with its hands
over its ears, singing stupid songs. Only the flicker
of the coat, the old man approaches statuary.

There is a concrete balustrade that surrounds
the plot of ground. Its supports are a set
of withered concrete urns around which
the squirrels chased each other all afternoon.

The trifles of the twilight flit and twitter
through the branches. Their foolish songs
nourish nothing but drifts and emotional
blanks of snow. The torpor of thickening amber.

This liquid light dissolves the categories of the will.
The day was a gorgeous urn decorated like a child
that will not share its toys. Upon the urn were painted
two dying men who could not touch each other.

The old man's breathing was a catch in his voice,
while I hovered, afraid of his disease.
His body, my body, have become an urn that can
only carry the ashes of the heart, the heartless.

First Break of Spring

You woke from that dream again,
to listen to a stiff wind
break panes of glass.
In the dark of the cottage,
air still smells of winter's sting.

You rose to walk the lake,
but the expected frisk
of water was lost
behind a wreck
of jagged ice.

The night storm
had piled slabs and chunks
along the beach, reaching
six feet in some places.
What is the strength

of water to discard
its crust into a scrum
of ice? It is Maya's palace.
Sunbeams enter,
and there, confused

by facets, bump
into the unseen wall,
dart through hopeless corridors,
stand in the invisible
pool of water.

The better half of memory
is your god, recollected
from the crackling surfaces
of thought and heaved
upon the shore of thinking.

The Authority of Roses

There are no roses but red ones.
The fragrance of a rose permeates
all of our thoughts about roses.
It confuses us to think on its odor.
The thorn of a rose, however, is not
the thorn of a problem. We know that
the problem of a rose has no solution.
Are we to consider white roses as roses?
The folding petals of a rose contain
the bud of an idea, the idea of a rose,
but that is not what I mean. I have no idea,
but the prick of the thorn on my thumb
produces a petal of blood. It stings!
We could follow the question of a rose
into its thicket and find there a damp
crumble of earth. Beneath the visible
is a kind of underground breathing,
made possible by worms. The metals,
however, that are good for the rose,
feed also the parasitic mildew.
By careful pruning we can promote
the growth of a shapely rose bush,
a bush that seems to burn with roses.
We cannot control the proliferation
of roses, the belief in their beauty,
the joy of a white rose, and its
rosy contradiction. Regardless
of how in our study we make
the ethereal ascent to genus and species,
we are drawn downward in amazement
at merest garden varieties. It appears
that our questions clip the roses
from their twigs. Yet we can go inside,
cleverly arrange them into a sprightly
bouquet, a display that fascinates
in the suffusion of a sweet smell.

Wedding Poem

For Leah and Elliott Malamet

You stand on the banks of a river
that unwinds toward the sea of salt.
The lucidity of its passage, the singularity

of its flow toward what it knows best,
these are its solemn characteristics;
they allow you to mark its placid

conveyance of the time you stand
together. Then a cross-wind ruffles
the surface and small waves run

backward obliquely, dizzying breezes
worry the water, fluttering forward
and back like the throat of a singer,

but also light carousing through the dark
and bright moments of a thirst for sound,
for the babble of a current that is tugged

and combed into life. Like a canopy cloth,
now you have a texture whose ripples
say more than they can ever tell.

One Gives Way

For Jeffery Donaldson

In the deadlocked heat
of summer's breathy mumble
one leaf can bear no more
and tumbles

into shimmered grass.
For now, the innocent
maple will not notice
one absent

tuft of furnished space.
Turn one leaf for another
in this our commonplace
book. Farther

into autumn's varnish,
branches concealed by leaving
give way to an empty slip's
revealing.

II.

Raining Cats and Dogs

The Beauty of It

This machine has its immobile intelligence.
Not the startled, crafty genius of deer
nor the contemplative tumble a river
ponders in its slow roil toward flatness.

Minnows are a microprocessing of sunlight
and deer will stand on their hind legs to reach
the uppermost tender leaves of philosophy.
The machine is all surface, whose meditation

is a pixilating play of sunlight across the tossing
water. This river of light has its shimmer of
spellbound intelligence. When the breeze shifts,
it freezes, then leaps into a forest of words.

The Dark Fruit of a Cosmology

Blackberries do suggest an explosion,
each hairy polyp thrusting the whole berry
toward the curving limits of space-time.
On the bush, they come in galaxies that spin
through the ethereal leaf, imprinted in green
light. Of course, we like to think of the present
as having more being than the future or the past,
the ripe produce dangling into its burnished weight.
Light-years distance these black nuggets
from the density of originary primordial jam,
as if they were spilled from a jar where gravity
collapses them toward incalculable quantum
uncertainties. As we find them today, the bang
of the berries exists in the watering bigness,
the mouth-rasping bundles of consumable
juice. The serrations of the vegetal expanse
are designed to confuse vision, to bend light
in and around the brakes and spiring canes,
but to tuck the leaves up is to expose clusters
of dark matter made succulent in the collisions
of the natural accelerator. Taste fires across
the roof of the mouth like photographic traces
of the sub-atomic flash, this is why we thrill to
these particles that have color, charm, and flavor.

The New Jersey Prickly Pear

One ear close to the ground, an elephant's ear,
and in the hunkering curve of the dune
and the beach plum and bayberry bent
over it is the elephantine body contorted
in just the way necessary for an elephant
to keep its ear pressed closely to the ground.

Keeping elephants watered is an enterprise
of sea and sky and convection that hurtles
immense cauliflower clouds that dampen
the air and plash through the strands of hair
on the back of a listening beast bewildered
by drops as thick as the humps of spiders.

As it drips through chaotic leaves it gathers
green into pebbles that drop into puddles
of wax. The splash hardens in a mold
whose wisdom holds the water, self-contained
and modest to a fault. The floppy apron is
residue of guttering candles of rain burnt-out.

It listens to the gurgle that drains the sand
toward a level we call an aquifer while it clings
to the cold in what seems to be a desert's waste
without the desert's blistering extremes.
This is the pear with a prick of elephantine
memory, not the gorgeous yellowy bell.

Travels in Greece

Each time you go somewhere, it is not
where you want to go. Zeno realized this.

'Go only half way,' he said.
The Aegean brings us to a standstill.

So many islands, but which one?
The barques in a breeze release the moan

of our desire to move. 'Lovely day for a visit,'
Heraclitus, while bathing, once remarked.

Chunks of canvas puff in and out like lungs.
'Air is the element above all others.'

'Inspiration and expiration,' states Anaximenes,
his principled torso chisel-nosed and statuary.

Sandwiches unpack themselves from wax paper.
Salad days and a new recipe called 'Feta Complete.'

Someone is sure to suggest Troy, as if our rituals
were victorious ruins. We went there last year.

Someone has a friend in Paphos, but I didn't
come here to gamble away my provisions.

Someone mentions the women in Egypt.
Thales is in for a swim. He calls,

'The water's great.' Empedocles is in a fight,
pounding his optimistic fists into flesh.

It was only yesterday that he told me,
'there is no glass too empty or too full.'

Two or three guys have gotten out their lyres.
Old Parmenides gabbling about oneness and dream.

His recent travelogue states: 'Why bother?
All motion is illusion.' They're down

in the field with their bows, practicing hamartia.
There hasn't been a cloud in the sky all week.

There come some out of the woods, returning from lunch
Anixamander thinks the sun is sucking the life out of us.

The remainder of our holidays slipping away,
the earth as dry as baked horse turds.

Seems like it's time to be moving on,
with the islands laid out ahead of us like atoms.

The sea glitters and falls. That's Democritus' boat
circling past the first visible ochre cliffs.

Pan-Hellenic Montréal

For Allan Garshowitz

Another Mercurochrome morning, one's breath
   the palpable helmet of Athene, the daily
bread and the tuna between it (things haven't changed
   since they tore down the Gai Apollon),
the motile personages stamp pneumatically
   to their employment. Not mountebank:
porched on the bank of a royal mount –
   muezzin to my quintuplicated homage:
bow wow. The sun descends in a column
   of which you are the apophyge.

In another season, the apologue would squirt
   from the fountain (in French?) of wisdom:
a fox, some grapes – not sour. As we stem christie
   through our days, a daze of light splashes
just as we always suspected it would – forgive
   my princely hectoring, I'm pierced
with a well-spoken arrow. The already common
   types are in their chase making an impression
on a page (message boy). Consider this homophyly
   freely given, fleur-de-lys, a filiation.

Now Hear This

How is it possible, plump plum or
bare branches, the thud of the apples
falling, blue sky, serious wisping
of cirrus, thunderous excavations,
Pre-Cambrian Shield, carapace
of the core, throbbing liquefactive
streams of molten metals?
Center and circumference are not
to be believed when there is no
compass, no encompassing embrace,
like trying to reach your arms around
a giant redwood, so empty you can
drive a truck through it, if stars
blink in and out of existence like the
eyes of hippopotami, the wrinkly
skin of it, the bubbling soup.

Theory extends its hegemony;
the iron lung of the last week of July
in New Jersey, a jersey just purchased
at Penny's, is too simple, pure,
this polyester Pollyanna answer
over a rugose sack of skin.
Still, living in a temperate puff of air
that carries many fragrances of flowering
dogwoods and dogs in the woods –
not the gods, who stink only of sulphur
and phosphorous incandescence and
aspirations of burning and burning
and being unable to touch. For the
skin peels away in your nightmare,
or is it daydream, if everything lifts
in its glory, that divine mushroom.

Blustery Day

It wasn't that way in the beginning,
our logo printed lightly on the diaphaneity
of the day's exuberance like the escutcheon
we bear into the insignificant skirmishes
of an afternoon storm and its shivering pathos.
The clouds scoot in with the endless pities
presented or repealed with a rapidity
of flimsy newspapers scotch-taped against a sky.

A few leaves plastered to the sidewalk
by the rain's turbulence. A frenzied afternoon
of coffee and cream and the continual
stirring about in the espionage of our quotidian
selves, the disguises, the last-minute flights
to Cairo. Our apartments like the chambers
of government buildings and the negotiated
protocols, the office intrigues, the Xerox machines.

With a sudden craving for chicory salad
and mulled cider when the rain lets up,
some of us blow down to a café we know
whose neon lights now seem crisp as fresh carrots.
A perky waiter brushes up, gorgeous brooch
dangling from the escarpment of a lapel.
The rain glistens on the window like new tears
we might freely give to the heartaches of tomorrow.

Ionization
After Edgar Varèse's music 'Ionisation'

On the spiky lawn, the shoots splay
with idle vigor, the hose
slithers to a comic pulse in the flesh
of the palm. One hand twists the knurl
of a brass nozzle so as to squeeze the water
into a fine spray, sparkling its
cloud of gnats.

There is a sound
whose source cannot be identified,
that wavers like a siren
announcing the moment's emergency.
A red-winged blackbird pecking across
the grass for bugs, the denuded
forsythia rude in the garden strip
where the mud-daubers drone.

Imagine the careless power
that knows that everything here
is a send-up. Some maple seeds helicopter
into spider webs caught in the bushes.
A rocketing water splatters against
the side of your house.

III.

The Lake's Formality at Evening

Ephraim

For Rick Tibbetts – after Pontormo's 'Joseph in Egypt'

At the center is the stone, signifying
seven years of famine, against which
leans the omnipresent hooded figure.

One is impoverished, believing that the rock
is infirm, without issue. The special gift
given late has been destroyed by wild beasts.

You are the interpreter of this dream:
that seven fat were devoured by seven lean.
Above this scene the stone is carved

into presiding spirits: Cupid, Venus, Mars.
Cruelty, it seems, can bring forth providence,
the mighty storehouse of the grain.

Pharaoh accepts the pecunia of Israel
and settles the brothers into pastures:
I am as a pharaoh to you, and one weeps

into a brother's shoulder. Could Cupid
join the hanging flesh with a shaft of corn?
Did Venus sanction her season of plenty

with a season of despair? Can Mars extend
a fertile ear against the one that droops?
The hammered coins are found inside the sacks.

Time's progression has become unsettled,
the appropriate passage of one year
to the next. This is what you tell them

when they discover themselves in supplication.
I come round to you like the grinding stone,
our embrace disguised by the swelling loaf.

It is Israel's blindness that makes a gift
of what was stolen, passing the blessing
to the younger son by laws of affection.

After the fabulous stairs that lead to ruin,
Pontormo prepares a benediction,
brushing into hunger his adopted son.

The Unity of Art and Experience

For Eleanor Cook

I. We walk the winding path at cliff's edge
till we come to a spot marked by a stump.
From this prospect, the sublime is something

earthly after all. The dog sniffs at splintered
wood, listens to a rustle of air. The layers
of hill and sky repeat in ribbons of blue.

In Correggio's depiction, Ganymede
looks back with an expression of measured
fear and pleasure. His fingers gather around

a clutch of feathers, and he drapes one
complicit arm over the pinion, lifting
him to a surprise of being weightless.

It is the season for it, when you shoot
out of yourself and summer is at hand,
nothing in flight seems broken as a stump.

The fig tree is tender when it first unfolds
its leaves, in this time of feathered light
when you know no man but your father.

You might know summer, but in the kingdom
of a dog the stump still grapples with earth
in tendrils that twist into darkest pockets.

ii. I would call it a gravel road the way
   it unravels down from the hills behind
   the town to the houses where we live.

   We climb the hill on a summer evening
   to pick oranges and to commit to memory
   a sunset's pale discoloring of the wharf.

   According to Garofalo, we are
   Pallas Athene and Neptune guiding
   the useful arts – the horse against the olive.

   Naming the named thing, the finger that
   indicates what belongs to whom, for we
   belong to our city, as we call it.

   So this web is spun to tangle in it
   something of the gods and clinging to our
   threads their tears. They wash our feet

   and we forgive them most where most we owed.
   We cannot keep the oil against our burial;
   it glistens along the skin of our flesh.

   Every road is known by the fruit it bears,
   and by this knowledge I pluck an orange.
   Would you pick an orange, the olive, a horse?

III. The gaze through the binoculars focuses
on a segment of a sea-story, and though
the detail of the waves comes close to you

like a horse's teeth, like the dolphins
slinking through the troughs, it can only be
at the expense of staring him in the eye.

There on Galatea's upper arm, Raphael
cannot prevent a bruise of chipping paint
where Polyphemus roughly clutched her into life.

The brush of wind ripples the marble
surface of the sea-cloth across her thigh –
ideal beauty is stalked by one-eyed truth.

Time's arrows hold the darts of love,
and if you remember where you fell,
you have not forgotten first desire.

The conches and the trumpets sound
for a place where one must seek for death
and wonder why it flees across the waves.

You must withdraw your eye from the eyepiece,
for the scallop shells have wheels of poise,
and pudgy Eros reclines to his repose.

iv. Is this why we go out in the morning
    where the day can unfold and wrap its arms
    around us from both sides of the lane,

    where any one of these trees might be
    Vertumnus assuming his leafy guise
    to garner the fruit of Pomona?

    And so Pontormo's agreeable fresco
    may not be Vertumnus and Pomona –
    the subject doesn't read into the painting.

    Still, where else can you find a boy
    reaching for a slender shoot, his legs splayed,
    and his shivering dog stretched below?

    The plant and tree book presents more
    Latin names than can be absorbed –
    in the vertigo of turning pages

    Vertumnus is the spine, the contrapposto
    torso of the wood. How can we know
    against which tree to lay siege?

    By a rude tree we fix the absolute.
    Or we return to the freshness of the season,
    placing a hand gently on the extended branch.

v. Who would not wish to drift along the Arno,
   for its beauty is a woman's beauty,
   where its curves delineate a passage

   into nature, or into a city
   constructed from nature's advantages,
   walls in a distant circle of embrace.

   Gentility and ease are Daphne's
   in Pollaiuolo's portrait, Apollo's
   grace and anguish grafted into laurel.

   We thought we had it in our grasp, a shade
   of leaving; not passion, but its signal
   should we weave a wreath into its foliage.

   Do not say we are without affection,
   for the natural man will not behold
   the bounty of her spirit, or what she

   offers in the spray of her twiggy limbs.
   And doesn't nature teach us that she should
   be covered in the presence of a god?

   As if a breath of air that turns the leaves
   recalls, not stillness, but the sound of feet
   as she scampered from the river to the forest.

vi. On the opposite hills are the towns we
   might have visited, but here are we poised
   like the cocked ears of the rabbits poking

   from their burrows, startled and attentive,
   anticipating the spirits. We swept the ground,
   foreseeing the measure of their dainty feet.

   They form an unearthly chain of dreaming,
   as Mantegna sees them, these nine sisters
   touching hands, and swayed in a cyclical dance.

   To our surprise, they are conjured here
   not by shrunken Apollo, but Mercury Ascendant,
   who sheds the ducal joy in harmony

   of marriage through the arts. And didn't we
   know that love and strife were not contentious
   after all, when Mars and Venus preside,

   their arms entwined the way love covers sin,
   that he may do battle in his own person,
   that she may rest from the work she has done.

   Perhaps we could slink from this fantastic,
   back to the forge where hammered silver waits,
   the jugs and hardened bowls, the sculpted rock.

VII. Is it too much to have a weathered print
of Raphael's 'The School of Athens' taped
to the far wall of the sunporch, so that

as we enjoy the morning's pleasantries
Plato and Aristotle step toward us,
extending their arms? The excitement, yes,

but the heated crowd disturbs one's contemplation.
We look again over the moody garden –
in session: Signorelli's 'School of Pan.'

The mantle of stars dangles across his breast,
twin crescent moons are the wistful genii
of melancholy. Everywhere is beauty

figured, but he keeps companion two old men,
sagging stomachs, and slung with limping sacks
of wine. Music is an unnatural noise.

The figures slightly out of perspective
employ their own spaces, in the difficulty
of corrupt and corrected posture.

The flutes of the crickets and bird whistles
on this Sunday morning call at people to
sit down to eat and drink, or rise up to play.

The Water Garden

A placid surface conceals the grip of the river
that congeals on a humid day into the stillness
where the river fattens toward somnolence
by my home town. The heart of the day pumps
its deliberate thud and shimmers of insects buzz
above the dank clumps of lake weed that drift
casually down river. The spinner that dropped
into the current winds simply back to the boy's

hands. What makes this moment so replete
with the ache of that vivid pulse? The boy
drives the fishing rod down into the murk
and it bends hard: the water divides into two
coils and the foam delivers a subtle hiss.
Flowers bloom and immolate in that green.

The Quarry
For Bruce Bond

What was full choir in a season of sweat
now lingers in the notes of stray birds. A net
of flies hovers over the leafless brake
that in a clutch of sticks seems to undertake
concealment of the abandoned quarry pit,
supplier once to complacent homes that sit
on what were, in the shady summer of a town,
the entangled limpid streets we ambled down.

I didn't notice the untuning of the instruments
after the performance. There remain implements
of that demise – a decay of mushrooms, long-
suffering ferns, the pensive reeds, this song.
Astonishing the clarity of what one knows
by the limestone pool in which nothing grows.

Returning *

Start at the end and move backward, perversely,
maybe the gurgle of reversing falls being different,
interesting, a turning against the chirping of
mountain streams and their flowings and emptying out.
The swell up into brackish mud flats lifts curtains
of seaweed, sips and laps at the twilight sedge.
The boats bow and pitch on the afternoon brine.
Eventually all things become unmusical.

What is the red arc, thrusting freckled scales
to breed? A fly sharpens its wings in a dull buzz
on steely meshing. Curious voyeur and courier
de bois, listen, the clunk of the paddle on the gunnel.
Observe, it all moves rush to the neck of the funnel,
up the throats of rivers, the ineluctable tidal bore.

* The amassing volume of water at rising tide in the bottle neck of the
Bay of Fundy between New Brunswick and Nova Scotia causes such
natural phenomena as the reversing falls and the tidal bore, a wave
which moves up against the flow of small rivers like the Petitcodiac.

The Western Skies

This is a paradise of fools, these are glass
birds chirruping, and this trembling belly
is a final human motion in a petrified forest.
Is this the choice: petrification or putrefaction?
You take factions against me, dearest earth,
though I soften to the ripple of fickle grain
in summer wind, or the late plenitude of stars
like golden apples on a charred and leafless bough.

The ants that swarm on a discarded lump of jelly
doughnut are as beautiful as the opening of peonies.
I believe that. Picking up an odd shoe, dirty socks,
placing shirts on hangers like so many ghostly selves,
chewing on toast, I wonder who will watch over me
as I stumble into accumulating idiosyncrasies.

Meditation Upon a Line From Joyce Carol Oates

Clammy as the interior of another's mouth,
the river sucks your breath away and returns it
only when you come up for air in the afternoon's
omniformity of the park. When looking back down
at bulbous growth in the umber of inky currents,
the pulsing weeds are tongues that babble the sound
of their perpetual drowning. They release artifacts
of their vanishing culture in the surface flicker.

White is the color of the middle air and the sparkling
linen of the café. The truth of brown is in the cup
of milky coffee. We miss nuances under the trees,
the shades of burnt almond, doeskin, negro, dun.
Perhaps it is better to hold the slime of a weed
to your cheek and think air is water and water air.

The Music of the Spheres

A bird begins its song with an astute
appeal to the planets where they lie stung.
The body resonates, no other lute
is quite so well made or so well strung.
In such darkness, a shimmer of light
shatters as it is plucked by fingers
that rustle across a fretboard of sight.
If the playing stops, the music lingers.

The music was immediate, the silence
yet to come, infinite. It is the fade
of the vibrating strings, that interval
the length of a bird's life, the violence
of music's combustion, the simple grade
that leads down scales to its terminal.

King of the Ghosts
'Aliens have kidnapped and raped me. What year is this?'

Some trees tonight are impersonating Elvis.
Even now he is asleep at the Three Point Motel.
We want to believe in his protective innocence,
but some people are victims of hostile intents.
Some day beings may come from outer space,
but the truly alien are the stars themselves,
their vast numbers, the heavenly hosts.
No wonder I choose just one to wish upon.

The wind whistles like a hound. Under
the cool spotlight like a shower of snow
he steps in regal robes, begins to sing a song
I remember well. Go back to sleep, I say.
The creature pauses in the glimmer and replies,
'Hostes alienigeni me rapuerunt. Qui annus est?'

Songs of Troy Remembered *

A Disguise

There are many dreams but few remembered
and when at night I turn my thoughts over and
over the way flames fold over the embers
of a campfire, I know I am a stranger to this land.
No army has me now, but I come to rest
at the gates of Troy. Here once was the cry
of victory, the torches, an urgent request –
the return of our own incomparable beauty.

When I wake to a mid-morning cerulean sky,
my throat constricts with a longing for that color
which I believe to be the lucency of the eyes.
I lift from my bedclothes and let my fingers sift
through a scraggly mane, and though of duller
stuff, I think these days are presented as a gift.

* These sonnets are to be understood as spoken by a veteran of the
Greek campaign who has returned years later and is camping outside
the walls of Troy.

Songs of Troy ...

Apparitions

This morning I glimpsed a woman on the parapets
who was not beautiful; perhaps she had been crippled
in our ancient war. Is it possible that one never forgets
the vista, the violet clouds, or the way the water rippled
with the fleets? I looked again and she was gone,
and I watched the heat of the burnished stone radiate
in shimmering distortions of the air, drawn on
in currents that display whatever my mind creates.

The clouds hurry through their shades of aquamarine.
In the afternoon, when a cooler breeze prevails
and scampers across the crisp surface of the Aegean
as if a messenger has arrived; it is then the flags
might snap and the horsemen assemble into tales
of battle and lead a charge, decked in resplendent rags.

Memory

The water slaps the shore in an endless banter
retrieved by fishermen who shout jibes about
each other's prowess with a boat. They saunter
to and fro straightening nets and I begin to doubt
my own memories of the scalding shouts of men
whose blood drained from them like whey seeping
from sacks of cheese. I said nothing then.
Only in this cheerful light do I feel like weeping.

There is a sour smell of fish parts in the air.
The men push onto the water in yawls named
for their wives or lovers. They surge to where
the catch runs thick in the voluptuous brine.
The shadows of the boats shiver through the enflamed
sea. The tremulous fish dart into the darkened wine.

Songs of Troy ...

Cassandra

Agamemnon. The fish I caught yesterday hang
hooked on my thoughts of you. Your eyes
are shriveled olives. The wooden floats bang
against the hulls. The whining of the flies.
The fishermen leave the nets where they lie
and shove their catch toward the markets
in the town. No one speaks of war. To die
is to be wrapped dutifully in a Persian carpet.

This is why I return to this city that is no longer
angry. They would wonder what all the fuss
is about, if I showed myself to be a fish monger
casting shadow on so much that flowers.
What we have taken will never belong to us.
What you left behind is irrevocably ours.

The Sounds of the Present

The turmoil of the air presents a tempest
of clotted sea-birds that twist and waver there
uncertain as to how to come to rest
on uneven waters. Even that they dare
this plosive breathing surprises the shavings
of frothy water cut from a tempered sea.
Strands of seaweed suggest unspoken cravings
in the way they catch and flutter from the quay.

Some who listen too intently to the whistling
sense the stinging in their eyes and later find
that in the quiet they listen only to their listening.
The birds veer, dip, rise and ripple, they go
where the wind takes, knowing it will unwind
itself in wandering through the islands below.

Songs of Troy ...

The Wooden Horse

Sometimes one needs something more than sea and sky,
and so I walked to town. Older women gathering gourds
shuffled through the crowd, and in the hue and cry,
past the hawkers roasting bits of lamb and skewered
eggplant, I happened on a man who had beaten his horse
to death. Others, if they had seen him, might have spoken
of the way he prodded at the creature without remorse,
but those eyes seemed saddened to me, almost broken.

The soldiers depended on their horses to carry them furiously
into the sting and swelter, though the horses could not know
of the disaster toward which they were stampeded. Curiously,
it didn't matter, they gathered under banners and time again
coursed across the dust and attended to the blow by blow;
and so it was a horse that disgorged those wooden men.

IV.

Domestic and Alien Waters

The Albatross

Large bird, accept flight like a nun's habit,
slide from the craggy mud of your nest,
shrug off the water's ventilation,
glide there on thermal compression.

Ten or twelve feet across? Spread
your feathered sinew to the measure,
insinuate yourself between the layers
of cold and warm, the sediments of air.

Long-traveled gatherer of the sea's refuse,
veer to the sheer heights of ocean swell.
Not more than three feet from the water's
surface, swerve to the roads beneath.

Twenty-eight days without touch of land,
rarely a rustle of the wing to sustain you,
follow the tangled path of your going
as if a story unfolded in the folding waves.

Turning over in the churning waves
are bits of crab and the flesh of dead fish
that you snatch and semi-digest, to bring
back to the gawking beaks of the young.

Peregrinations of eight thousand miles,
the effortless distance of your travel and
no discernible pattern to your ellipse,
now return to the point where you started.

The Albatross on Land

I had thought of you mated to wind and sea
and to the flesh of the sea, the body's rumpled
self rolling back and back in its bedclothes,
a dreamer wrestling with the sinking fathoms.

Quick to the quiver of fish, a plunge
to the thick of it, a thumb and finger
extinguishing the candle that flickers like a
corpuscle in the body's darkened chambers.

But thrust into the stiff breeze a lump of rock
and a patch of sedge where you return to brood
on mud cakes constructed for the purpose.
The cliffs are slick with droppings.

From the craws the wind plucks screeches
and carries them through the grasses.
The wings won't stay shut, but hang crooked,
and bang like clattering shutters in a gale.

And here you find the tender stretch of necks,
the clack of beaks, the rising from the feet
and circling like a gavotte, a gallivant of half-
spread wings, the smoky under-color exposed.

Across the waters linger lights of the fabulous,
stuck to dark's fabric, the literal ships, far from
where you huddle in flocks, not domesticated,
but domestic, thinking of the sea's eternal noise.

Dragonfly

You can't see it. Then it appears
on the periphery of vision
in its pattern of evasive action
as if it were the imaginary target
of a video game. It tantalizes.
Just as you believe it remains
a mere glimmer of sunlight,
it pauses, larger than life,
in all of its alien thinginess.

It has a solidity.
It makes a loud thwack
on the windshield of your
speedboat, splashing its dollop
of life. It flew into your path.
More than one appear
as the ubiquitous helicopters
of Vietnam movies,
remarkably predatory.

Evolution is a process of miniaturization.
Consider the gimpy wings
of those fire-breathers.
These are lightning across the water.
Nevertheless, its size is its advantage
when feeding on the smaller gnats
that frequent the lake's surface.
Some creatures have grace,
it has the power dive.

The quick heavy dragonfly
when it lights upon a rock
has expansive slight wings that
suggest the crackle of dried
maple seeds. It won't come near you,
won't brush by you like a butterfly.
To hold it in your palm would be
to hold the weight of its history. It lifts,
hovers, and then it's gone.

Mourning Doves

If they had elbows and forearms, they would be Rodin's
'The Thinker,' yet they are classified as game birds
by the federal government and thirty-one states.
When you wake in the morning, there is one
in the branch, seemingly still asleep,
though if you look long you notice the occasional
twitches of its head. Everywhere else
there are rituals of survival and propagation.
When dissected, the stomach of one contained
7,500 seeds of yellow wood sorrel; another,
6,400 of foxtail grasses. Perhaps the mourning dove,
named *zenaida macroura* by Charles Lucien Bonaparte
in honor of his wife the Princess, is aware of its nobility.
You are surprised by the strength with which they fly,
swift and plosive like a small hawk, with a musical
whistling of wings. Sometimes in winter they roost
at night on the ground (see *Toughness of a Bird's Feet*).
Is it indolence, then, or thoughtfulness, with which their
feathers nestle into a deep sloth? We have much to learn
about the way the male brings twigs to the female,
the way both sexes incubate the eggs equally,
perhaps even about the way they mate for life.
Do not ask for whom they mourn.

On the Death of a Cat

The problem: to expiate this smaller sorrow
that will not contain the fullness of grief.
Perhaps the way you licked methodically
at fleas, with a degree of patience,
when evening stepped across the yard.

Lavished with the name Sosostris,
whiskers told of what you had in common
with catfish. It is not you that's missed,
but only the scratch you made in our affections.
When called you would not come.

You bristled at the possible companion
suspected of being your replacement.
Impossible. While you lived,
you made savannah of a carpet,
created Swaziland behind the sofa.

Still, when there are no ears
to listen to the sounds of subtler life
scuttling beneath the floorboards,
this is a truly empty house.
I remember your weight against my shin.

The Natural Moose

This forest is coextensive with the mind's
expanse of spruce and pine and snow. Through it,
the moose meander mechanically in uncanny
circular tracks, following the map of their antlers'
tedious pointing. And here they come again
in an eternal return through space already occupied
by their previous going, until – you stop dead
to see one by the side of the road – it has entered
your map of asphalt disappearing over the hills.
What is your name and what are you called,
it seems to say, and how did you bring me here.
The crown of thorns lacerates your passing.
Is there an 'acrid odor'? Is it 'original response'?
But the night is as cold as white china and the air
is a dinner plate with a fine-edged crack. The moose
disappears back into its habit, and one night
as you stand at the sink washing dishes the phantom
moose vanishes, so you drop the plate. It lands on an edge
and circles back on itself; it doesn't break, the spruce
arched in the dark, and the pine thinking itself alone.

Squirrel

He scampers across the windowsill,
stops,
cocks his head.
'Hello,' he says,
'May I bury my nuts in your potted plants?'

Clouds funnel and twist,
crisp whistling in the twigs.
The first snow settles like fur.
He might sleep for a very long time
or he might chatter at us from a perilous branch.

'Hey! Looking for me?'
Hanging
or clinging to bark,
a tail coils or uncoils,
always a tree between us.

Tiny fingers scurry from limb to limb
or burrow to a bare necessity,
throbbing with questions.
He canters along the electrical wire,
as if receiving shocks.

When the garden is white,
he forgets where he put things,
but in his absentminded dreams
he believes that what he looks for
grows in another field.

In Order to Stalk a Groundhog

You will agree that they are adorable
for their awkwardness. If they hear
you after your first three steps, they trundle
into the bushy shadow. To get near

the groundhog, you must recall the skills
of red-light, green-light. This bundle
of grease and gristle dandles its head
in and out of the grass, sprawled in a tumble

of dandelion. No problem, you think, as the snout
disappears. When he pokes up, you stand dead
still. Down again and you tip-toe, stork-like,
one step, two steps, and freeze. He is well-fed,

you note, but he nibbles nervously and listens,
while you, foot extended, pretend you might
be thinking of tying your shoelace. Surprisingly,
you can stop-go in this fashion until you are right

next to him. Now you are aware that he knew
of your presence all along. Even when he
rubs his nose with his paws he watches you,
deliberates, then waddles spontaneously

to a safe distance. You are enjoying this game,
for in his casually studied behavior is a clue
to your diurnal habits, to your nervous munching,
to the way you two-step shuffle the way you do.

v.

The River That Winds Through Memory

First Visit to the Library

Shy, with hands stashed in pockets,
he regards the rows of shiny spines.
The armored light is prehistoric –
the enveloping hush of a 'Please be quiet.'
This is the old fire hall at Pine Point;

the sun twirls down slippery shafts,
dusts itself in a lemon-slice lattice.
Knowledge, he knows, lies in the encyclopedias
in banks in the center of the room,
like puffins on the cliffs of the bird islands.

Along the walls – his heart stops, and starts again –
are the mysteries. He picks *The Discovery
of the Skeleton Key*. He pauses in the shadows:
Little Women by Louisa May Alcott,
which makes him think of little peaches.

Books do and do not contain his loves.
He clambers onto a step ladder reaching
for Tom Swift. She says, 'Careful,'
from behind the large desk. She wears
a tartan skirt with a large safety pin.

The first time he understands his own name is
writing it on library slips, papers scattering
like bread crumbs in the backyard. The weight
of the books under his arm is comfortable.
Life, he suspects, will stretch out in a long line.

Forbidden Berries

For Anne Leckie

Do not concern yourselves with who ate first,
or who talked whom into what. With our little
puffy hands, we both reached out and plucked
the somewhat bland and sometimes sweet or slightly sour
fruit. It is with just such glee that conspirators act,
like Rosencrantz and Guildenstern, in a conspiracy
larger than themselves, that spins its unpleasant turns.

There by the garden path was the unusual bush,
the thrill of its intricate thickets and black
glossy berries. With its promise of night and fire
and the beauty of celestial pinwheels and showers
of stars, we stood amazed, my sister and I.
We paused under a slate-grey morning sky,
awakened from our play, alert to a tang of salt air.

Called for lunch we marched without respite
toward the clap of the screen door and confessed
right there in the kitchen next to the buckets
of blueberries waiting for washing. Mother was furious.
'You might never see me again, you know. It can be like that.'
Dread was the paralysis that tip-toed through the blood,
though she admitted later they weren't poisonous.

In the late afternoon quiet, confined to that secretive gloom,
I stared dumbly at the flowering grain and whirlpool knots
in the paneling of my room. Then, opening my favorite atlas,
picking over the pinks, reds, the purples and pale blues
of far-off countries and their black-starred capitals,
I sobbed. What did I know of the world's vagrancies?
I wished that I had never eaten those berries.

The Future at Seven on Shediac Beach

Until then you had constructed sand castles,
but early one morning an oily puff of smoke
arose from beyond the edge of the sea. Your eyes
locked to it as if it were the sign of an unknown
covenant. A sea-going vessel emerged from the deep.

Your ship came in. The warmth a boy feels for
his father can be measured on such evenings
of a promised visit to the wharf. The weather-beaten
trawlers dip and sway; their engines sound precisely
like a boy's first growling imitation of an engine.

Oily men who smell of brine clatter large crates
of lobster onto the planks of the dock. The creatures
clamber on each other. A jovial man plucks one deftly
around the abdominal plate and waves it toward
your face. Another has his hand wrapped in bandages.

Last week this is all the excitement you required.
Now it is overshadowed by the freighter your father
tells you is registered in Liberia. Large roaring funnels
dangle over the railings pouring grain into giant
containers. You let sand trickle through your fingers.

Your father tires quickly and offers a long drive.
An hour passes when you arrive at the end of a point.
The sea has grown angry. Billowing clouds churn
motionlessly in the air. A black veil restrains
the sky. Later that night, the storm doesn't break.

Shediac Beach, New Brunswick
For Robert B. Leckie

Follow the narrow path through the spike grass
to the edge of the bluffs and note the catch
in your throat at the summer's first sight
of a stark sky and the metallic green glitter.

Remember as you walk to feel again the damp
dryness of the sand upon your feet and the screech
of gulls, the reek of dead or decomposing fish
that lift and settle with each wave at shoreline.

If you lunge to the surf the water grapples with you.
Some slimy weeds brush your stomach as you swim
to the first sandbar that forms a protective shell for
the amniotic pool through which scuttle nervous crabs.

Now swim on to the second sandbar, always submerged,
and test its existence by the trust of your descending feet.
Stand suspended waist-deep in agitated waters,
as if by magic, then look back at the distant strand.

Could you have been so lonely in the fat afternoons
with your mother and sister plucking blueberries
into a plastic bucket, bruising a bluish tinge
into your hands, or into the sable evenings

of whispered conversations and the shuffling of cards,
the whine of the space heater and its electrified
glowing red filaments? In the night you hear
the voices of neighbors from closely-packed cabins.

You think there is one boundary that you cross
as you grow up, from the toss and turn of the sea
one sharply dividing shore delineated by
the constant wash and splash of memories.

Consider the perpetual drift of jellyfish
that follow in nameless communities where
tides drag them, pulsing their transparent
carcasses and trailing their undulant tendrils.

Growing Up Anglo in Québec

As a young boy you sidle up to a table
in the restaurant and wonder how
they can talk without saying anything.
Such is the subtle service of power
that their intimacy is on display for you.

La porte, la fenêtre, these are the rudiments
of a guttural culture. The very way in which
you are made to learn them is to display
that you are not what they are. It is to be spoken
as if the mouth were full of bitter chocolate.

You are to understand the word for word
of authority in the exercise of *La Dictée*.
Let us review the names by which we know them best:
pea soup, pepper, Pepsi, Mae West, frog.
They are known to have bad teeth.

Pea soup: a viscous liquid high in fat content
and carbohydrates. Pepper: a black,
granular powder that causes a burning
sensation to the tongue. Pepsi: also dark,
an effervescent beverage made of root

extracts, quantities of glucose, carbonated
water and preservative chemicals.
Mae West: the brand name of a small cake
wrapped in white-and-yellow cellophane,
filled with yellow icing and coated with semi-

sweet chocolate. Frog: a tailless, aquatic,
leaping amphibian whose croak sounds
like a thumbnail flicked on the teeth
of a comb. They come from the muck
and they return to the muck. They are oily.

We conquered them on the Plains of Abraham.
They ran across the grasses, firing wildly.
In two volleys, we slaughtered them.
We remind ourselves that we maintained discipline
by lighting firecrackers on Victoria's Birthday.

Because they believe in incense and the Pope
they are not allowed to teach us the way they speak
in the Protestant School Board of Greater Montreal,
who hired Americans to teach us 'Parisian French.'
Fortunately they all speak a species of English.

As a young boy I clutched the stone, listened
to the light breathing of my comrades and our
rustling in the bushes where we waited for them.
We were separate, wanted to be separate, yet
we became so angry when they spoke of separatism.

Removing the Long Grass

The flies were at their worst the summer we worked
on the grounds crew of that old hotel. Well-heeled
old men clinging to their past mingled on the porch
and fingered the mountains that leaned close to us.

To our surprise, the splinter-handled scythes
were easy in their weight and sprung into the grass
by a simple dip and bob of the hips. A meadow
breeze echoed the sound that we made there.

The hotel carried its past like a persistent dream
of bronze fire-extinguishers, spring water
tapped from mountain creeks, the hiss and
tumble of embers turning in a wood furnace.

A pair of women sipping lemonade on a verandah
stretching into shadows in either direction sat
blankly looking into the summer heat. We swung
at the grass in an effort to save the picturesque.

We were only boys, too young to be much impressed
with scythe-sound or the rasp of the blades as they sliced
an indiscriminate path through the various weeds.
Flies hummed, and we sang the top forty all afternoon.

The Lost Orphanage at Montfort
For Gary Geddes

Strolling by lakeside at dusk, two stars
poke out like the eyes of animal night.
There are reflections, shimmering.
They replace what lies below,
the gloom inhabited by fish.

Ripples whisper on the water
and the fiery scallop shells of clouds
undulate with the chromaticism
of daylight in a distant land. It is only
at this moment that one observes the cross,

naked, etched out amongst the trees,
stooping on the well-rounded hill,
marking the lost orphanage at Montfort.
Turning back, it is the immense dark
and tangible cold that surprise.

Last light itemizes the remaining images
I might carry home: the placid waxy
green of the lily pads, two or three
individual spruce and their black,
ice-sharp needles. I pick up

a rough, burnt-out cinder, a relic
of the old railroad. How is it,
in the singularity of this metamorphic dark,
that there exists this aching continuity?
I walk as I walk, as long as there is locomotion.

Frenchman's Bay, Lake Ontario

The pleasure craft slip through the lake's
creamy reflections like lubricated condoms.
Their unibody constructions are laminated
with the gorgeous gradations of plastic decor:
vinyl, latex, Plexiglas and polystyrene.
Listen to their engines' muffled 'I sing.'

The water ruffles its feathers like an aquatic
bird in the late afternoon breezes that signal
the end to an afternoon's vicissitudes. The sail-
boats furl their canvas and their brightly-colored
flags stiffen into banners of gratification and
the plump primping priapism of their masts.

As the gloom gathers, the boats come from
every direction to this small harbor. One feels
desire stirring again as one gazes at the pixels
of the over-sized television screen of night.
A few stragglers throb home from beyond
the horizon and the United States of America.

Leaving New Jersey

This diversity fares well without my wishes.
Consider dogwood in the native and the Japanese
varieties. The native blossoms first, of course,
in stark implosions along the clotted twigs
that wind beneath the oaks. The Japanese
attends its clothing, then jewels itself
in petals of reticent yellow. The native dogwood,
for all its efforts to jump the gun, greets inseparable
flowering fruits and bushes, only some of which
I can actually name. After this miscellany,
New Jersey becomes briefly foreign, subdued
by a rounding out in quiet shades of green.
When it is most uniform, it is least itself.
Before long, however, fireflies begin their
incendiary flights. The heat arrives.
Everything grows to a size larger than it should be.
Even the air swells and bulges against the sky.
Clothing becomes damp and heavy, like
the hug of an aging aunt. It is not as if
it is autumn elsewhere. It's not. Yet New Jersey's
way of sticking close to you is like memory,
tensile, complicated, then soft suggesting rot.

What Happens There Happens Here

The damping of sound by the gathering
kerfuffle of snow creates an eerie shadow of regret,
like leaving the summer property by the lake
one last time after your father has sold it.
Can you remember the rock bass
leaping into the evening calm,
chasing after insects skiffling over the water's
surface like these snowflakes falling now?
Until it is pinned by snow and its accumulating
weight, a scrap of cellophane suggests
the rattle of a storm not heard.
Interesting that, when by itself,
scampering about the yard,
it is a brief and insubstantial thing,
like the bats that used to flit
among the branches of the cedars
in that twilight so long ago.
Now that it is caught in a snatch of snow,
it surfaces into billows like a winter ghost of the way
a bass could thrust from a placid lake of memory
and splash into the radiating rings of remembrance.
It is not a nostalgia for the absent child,
nor the familiar pang of a known place
given over, nor even the acknowledging
of an empty satchel of transient desire.
After all, your father offered to keep the place
so you could do with it as you pleased,
sometime down the road. Before dawn,
someone has left the tracks of his vanishing,
then dematerialized in this material air;
and perhaps it is only this, not the mutability
of a human life, but the way it is self-effacing,
marked by the mere hint of a direction
that even now is being smoothed over and filled in,
the cold prints disappearing like a cousin once-removed.
From behind these winter windows it seems

like a miracle of silence, looking over an expanse
of time to nothing, really, just a thought, a gesture,
the gesture of a moment that maintains a strange
affiliation through a turbulence of self-forgetting,
the drift and banking of everything you once wanted
and can't have, something that sparkles in the air,
something like a person who waited just a moment
before passing on, and you think they glanced
in your direction, even nodded once, yes, nodded
once or twice, and then you could think about
everything that's broken, that history itself,
with its crooked back, its twisted joints, limped
into this yard and lay itself in humps under the snow.
We called the place Lake Massawippi,
which we never tired of spelling backwards,
though now I can spell neither backwards nor outwards,
watching the alphabet of snow as it tumbles
in its exaggerated but agreeable and friendly wave
toward a language which, if we spoke it, would sound,
as I have already said, something like regret.

The Reunion
For Karen Dowker

The train pulls into a small station
in the early morning. From my upper
berth, I can see we are on the prairie.

The rails do not meet at the horizon.
'Death was instantaneous,' someone says,
and how could it be otherwise, unless

it is forever figured in everything
I can see to the horizon, plus
everything I can see in every horizon

afterwards. I'm not a farmer,
but the grain looks ready for harvest –
bushels and silos, the emotional life.

Doesn't it always? Look ready,
that is – which is why I know these people
milling about the platform and why

a hardened rail runs through our lives,
forwards and backwards, and when we
arrive where we started, it's a leafy

eastern suburban accumulation
of the good life, as strange as China,
and as familiar as the home we always

wanted. In the instant the train pulls out,
the horizon changes, is changed, we change,
and the grain wavers in its expected way.

Flying North

The sun tumbles behind you toward a curvature
while the plane arrows into the silent vicissitudes,
the snow tumbling and baffling, like a manifold
of hibernation. It is as if there has been an evacuation
of the now, an arching back and forward to the past
and to the future. To come to these acceptable
wooden houses patched to a place of endless trees.
It is a garrison and trading post; it is a sentinel
in deepest space listening for signs of intelligent
life. It is the last bastion of the ordinary.
You have come so far to have come only half way
into the polar night and the calling that is yours.
Except that you didn't call and nothing called you,
and nothing but the thrum of the engines
and the scrape of the ice in the plastic glass
into which a steward has poured some coke.
You might give up reading for a bit, for the landscape
is opaque and textured and glazed or whitened
or etched or none of the above – it is unstoried.
No, the stories are told again and again, and they
are simple stories of arrival and departure, of coming
and going, of moving about and over, of the migration
of species, of the snow snaking across a lake.
Yes, it is a story of completion and incompletion,
of landing in a place you could call almost home.

The Wheelchair
In Memory of Robert G. Leckie

To compensate for the body's weakness,
it is full of nifty springs and levers
that click and slide metallic armatures
into gentle positions of support.

Its fluting pipes glitter with shiny
utopian cleanliness, like the miniature dream
of some long-gone industrial epoch.
The whistle of the vinyl as it

accordions open is almost like breathing;
a breath sucked in surprise at a surprising
agility, or its lack. So too
the effortless wheels that spin easily

augur no fortune; no giddy heights
or plunging despair. Only the handles
in their subtle tug suggest the weight
of a body and its useless appendage.

But they do so in a perfect caress
without touch, that transmutes pain
into the nubs and knuckles of the plastic
grips by which I hold you, move you.

A sedentary day of casual words unraveled,
let this serviceable metaphor wheel us
through one more turning, by which I bring
you to a bed, and another round of sleep.

Acknowledgements

Some of these poems appeared originally in *American Literary Review, The Antigonish Review, Ariel, Denver Quarterly, Descant, The Fiddlehead, The Greenfield Review, The Kelsey Review, The New Republic, Southwest Review,* and *US1 Worksheets.*

I am grateful to John Donlan, editor at Brick Books, for his interest in and patience with this book.

This book would not have been possible without the editing, friendly suggestions, and general support of the following people: Annette Abma, Bruce Bond, Eleanor Cook, Jeffery Donaldson, Allan Garshowitz, Gary Geddes, Jennifer Gustar, Richard Howard, Gerry Jackson, A.F. Moritz, John Reibetanz, Kathryn Taglia, and Frederick Tibbetts, as well as members of the US1 Workshop and the Toronto Writing Group.

The photo of the author was taken by Rob van Adrichem.

Biographical Note

Ross Leckie was born in Lachine, Québec, and still thinks of Montréal as home. He studied English and Philosophy at McGill University and Education at University of Alberta, before taking a Creative Writing Masters at Concordia University and a Ph.D. in English at University of Toronto. He has published essays on modern and contemporary poetry, contemporary American fiction, and cultural studies.

His poems have appeared in such journals as *The Antigonish Review, Ariel, Descant, The Fiddlehead, Denver Quarterly, The New Republic, Southwest Review,* and *American Literary Review.* His first collection of poetry, *A Slow Light,* was published in the Signal Editions series of the Véhicule Press.

He lives in Prince George, British Columbia and teaches English Literature and Creative Writing at the brand new University of Northern British Columbia. He has a strong interest in cultural theory, and one can usually find him listening to music or watching film.